Snakes

Debbie Gallagher

Marshall Cavendish
Benchmark
New York

This edition first published in 2010 in the United States of America by Marshall Cavendish Benchmark
An imprint of Marshall Cavendish Corporation

Website: www.marshallcavendish.us

This publication represents the opinions and views of the author based on Debbie Gallagher's personal experience, knowledge, and research. The information in this book serves as a general guide only. The author and publisher have used their best efforts in preparing this book and disclaim liability rising directly and indirectly from the use and application of this book.

Other Marshall Cavendish Offices:
Marshall Cavendish Ltd. 5th Floor, 32-38 Saffron Hill, London EC1N 8 FH, UK • Marshall Cavendish International (Asia) Private Limited, 1 New Industrial Road, Singapore 536196 • Marshall Cavendish International (Thailand) Co Ltd. 253 Asoke, 12th Flr, Sukhumvit 21 Road, Klongtoey Nua, Wattana, Bangkok 10110, Thailand • Marshall Cavendish (Malaysia) Sdn Bhd, Times Subang, Lot 46, Subang Hi-Tech Industrial Park, Batu Tiga, 40000 Shah Alam, Selangor Darul Ehsan, Malaysia

Marshall Cavendish is a trademark of Times Publishing Limited

All websites were available and accurate when this book was sent to press.

Library of Congress Cataloging-in-Publication Data

Gallagher, Debbie, 1969–
    Snakes / Debbie Gallagher.
        p. cm. — (Zoo animals)
    Includes index.
    Summary: "Discusses snakes, their natural habitat, behavior, and
    characteristics, and zoo life. "—Provided by publisher.
    ISBN 978-0-7614-4749-8
    1. Snakes—Juvenile literature. 2. Captive snakes--Juvenile literature.
    3. Zoo animals—Juvenile literature. I. Title.
    SF408.6.S63G35 2010
    639.3'96--dc22
                                                2009039867

First published in 2010 by
MACMILLAN EDUCATION AUSTRALIA PTY LTD
15–19 Claremont Street, South Yarra 3141

Visit our website at www.macmillan.com.au or go directly to www.macmillanlibrary.com.au

Associated companies and representatives throughout the world.

Copyright © Debbie Gallagher 2010

Edited by Georgina Garner
Text and cover design by Kerri Wilson
Page layout by Raul Diche
Photo research by Legend Images
Base maps by Gaston Vanzet, modified by Kerri Wilson

Printed in the United States

Acknowledgments
The author and the publisher are grateful to the following for permission to reproduce copyright material:

Front cover photo of an Emerald tree boa © Joe McDonald/ AUSCAPE

Photographs courtesy of: © Joe McDonald/AUSCAPE, 1; Bristol Zoo Gardens, 21; © Image Source/Corbis, 27 (right); © Sly/Fotolia, 3, 6; Justin Sullivan/Getty Images, 4; Knoxville Zoo, 24, 25; Legendimages, 16, 17, 26 (left and right), 27 (left); © Gunther Schmida/Lochman Transparencies, 30; Photolibrary/ Suzanne L and Joseph T. Collins, 20; Photolibrary/Zigmund Leszczynski, 23; Photolibrary/Morales, 11; Photolibrary/John Nees, 19; Photolibrary/Tony & Sheila Phelps, 22; Photolibrary/ Dr Morley Read, 18; Photolibrary/Austin J Stevens, 7; Rob Cruse Photography, 12; © ananas/Shutterstock, 8 (snake silhouette); © Alexander Chelmodeev/Shutterstock, 13; © Philip Date/Shutterstock, 5; © EcoPrint/Shutterstock, 15; © John Sartin/Shutterstock, 10; © Susan Flashman/Shutterstock, 14; Woodland Park Zoo, 28, 29.

Many zoos helped in the creation of this book. The authors would especially like to thank ZooParc de Beauval, France, Knoxville Zoo, USA, Woodland Park Zoo, USA, and Bristol Zoo Gardens, England.

While every care has been taken to trace and acknowledge copyright, the publisher tenders their apologies for any accidental infringement where copyright has proved untraceable. Where the attempt has been unsuccessful, the publisher welcomes information that would redress the situation.

Contents

When a word is printed in **bold**, you can look up its meaning in the Glossary on page 31.

Zoos

Zoos are places where people can see a lot of different animals. The animals in a zoo come from all around the world.

People can visit zoos to see animals from other parts of the world.

Zoos have special **enclosures** for each different type of animal. Some enclosures are like the animals' homes in the **wild**. They have trees for climbing and water for swimming.

Animals such as orangutans need trees for climbing.

Snakes

Snakes are **reptiles**. They have no arms or legs, and no outer ears. They smell by tasting the air around them with their tongues.

long body

eyes with
no eyelids

long
tongue

A snake is a long animal with no arms or legs.

There are more than two thousand different **species** of snake. Some snakes are long and thin, and some are large and thick. Some have a **venomous** bite.

The anaconda, from South America, is the largest snake in the world.

In the Wild

In the wild, snakes live in most parts of the world. They use the sun's heat to keep warm. Snakes cannot live in very cold areas such as Antarctica.

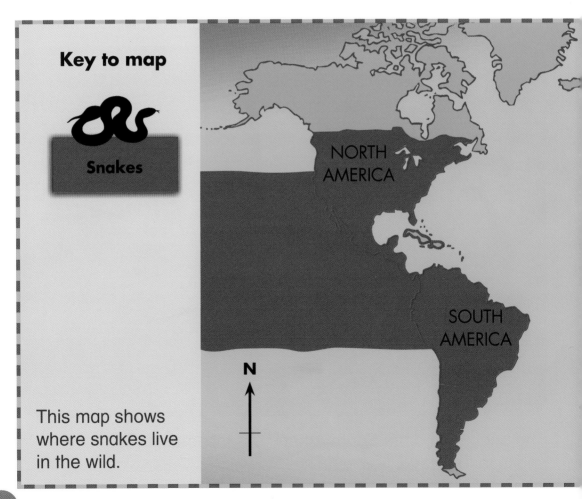

Key to map

Snakes

N

This map shows where snakes live in the wild.

Snakes live in most kinds of **habitats**. Some snakes, such as the king brown snake, live in hot deserts. Others, such as the yellow-bellied sea snake, live in the sea.

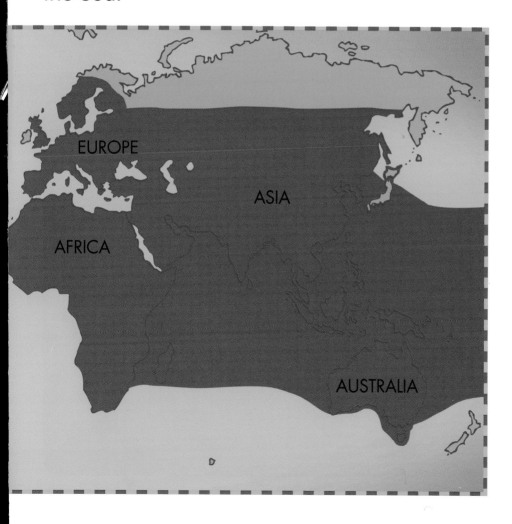

Threats to Survival

The biggest threat to the survival of snakes is the clearing of land. Land is cleared to build farms, roads, and towns.

This land, where snakes once lived, has been cleared for farming.

When land is cleared, snakes lose their natural habitats. They have fewer places to hunt for food. Snakes may be killed if they leave the cover of their habitats.

When trees are cut down, snakes that live in them lose their habitat.

Zoo Homes

In zoos, snakes live in enclosures. Snakes need the right temperature in their enclosures. Sometimes, zookeepers use a heating lamp in the enclosure.

heating lamp   trees for climbing

glass so visitors can see inside enclosure

This enclosure has a heating lamp that the snake can lie under.

Snakes need hiding places in their enclosures. Climbing snakes need trees. For some snakes the air in the enclosure also needs to be wet or damp.

Snakes need water in their enclosures for drinking.

Zoo Food

All snakes eat other animals and insects.
Zookeepers feed snakes dead animals and eggs.

In zoos, snakes are
fed whole mice.

A Snake's Zoo Food
mice
rats
chicks
eggs

Feeding

Zookeepers do not feed snakes every day. Snakes only need to eat every few days. Snakes cannot chew with their teeth and swallow their **prey** whole.

A snake opens its jaws wide and swallows a rat.

Zoo Health

Zookeepers clean the enclosures so that the snakes stay healthy. Once a week, the zookeepers remove everything from the enclosure. They clean everything and then put it all back.

Zookeepers give the snakes freshwater each day.

Snakes **shed** their skins up to ten times a year. The keeper makes sure their skin is healthy. They also check that the snakes' eyes are clear.

thermometer

Zookeepers use thermometers to check the temperature in the snake enclosures.

Baby Snakes

Most snakes lay eggs. The mother snake finds a warm place to lay her eggs. Most baby snakes, called hatchlings, look after themselves once they break out of their egg.

A nest of baby snakes hatches out of their eggs.

Nearly all sea snakes give birth to live babies and do not lay eggs. Some land snakes give birth to live babies, too.

Some baby snakes are born alive and not in eggs.

How Zoos Are Saving Snakes

Zoos help save **endangered** snakes. San Francisco Zoo is in California. It helps takes care of injured garter snakes before returning them to the wild.

San Francisco Zoo protects San Francisco garter snakes and their habitats.

Bristol Zoo, in England, is helping save the endangered Savu python through **breeding**. Some of the baby pythons are given to other zoos.

In 2003, nine Savu pythons were born at Bristol Zoo.

Zoos Working Together

Zoos work together to breed endangered snakes. North American zoos cooperate on Species Survival Plans. They keep records about certain species of snake.

Zoos work together on a survival plan for Aruba Island rattlesnakes.

These records are like a family tree. Zoos use the records to find snake breeding partners at other zoos. The snakes can be borrowed for a short time to breed.

California kingsnakes are bred under a species survival plan.

Meet Phil, a Snake Keeper

Phil works as a zookeeper at Knoxville Zoo, in Tennessee.

Question How did you become a zookeeper?

Answer I volunteered in the zoo before I applied for the zookeeper job.

Question How long have you been a zookeeper?

Answer I have been working as a zookeeper for thirteen years.

Phil carefully holds an Egyptian cobra.

Question What animals have you worked with?

Answer I have worked with reptiles and **amphibians**, but I especially love snakes.

Question What do you like about your job?

Answer I get to study snakes in the wild, too. This helps me learn how to better take care of snakes at the zoo.

A Day in the Life of a Zookeeper

Zookeepers have jobs to do every day. Often, a team of zookeepers work together to look after the snakes at a zoo.

8:00 a.m.
Check the schedule to see what the snakes need.

9:00 a.m.
Check all the snakes are healthy.

1:30 p.m.

Get bedding ready for the snakes to lay eggs.

3:30 p.m.

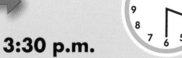

Talk to visitors about the snakes.

Zoos Around the World

There are many zoos around the world. Woodland Park Zoo is in Seattle, Washington. It has different types of snakes, such as anacondas, boa constrictors, and cobras.

A zookeeper moves around the climbing poles in the cobra enclosure.

Zookeepers at Woodland Park Zoo teach people about animals. There are talks, classes, and tours. Some visitors get to touch and hold the snakes.

A zookeeper introduces a boa constrictor to visitors at the Woodland Park Zoo.

The Importance of Zoos

Zoos do very important work. They:
- help people learn about animals
- save endangered animals and animals that are badly treated

Australia Zoo is breeding the endangered woma python.

Glossary

amphibians A group of animals that includes frogs and toads.

breeding Caring for animals so that they can produce babies.

enclosures The fenced-in areas where animals are kept in zoos.

endangered At high risk of dying out and disappearing from Earth.

habitats Areas in which animals are naturally found.

prey An animal that is hunted and killed for food.

reptiles A group of animals, such as snakes and crocodiles, with dry, scaly skin.

shed To get rid of skin and replace it with new skin.

species Groups of animals or plants that have similar features.

venomous Containing venom, a liquid poison that can harm or kill.

wild Natural areas, such as forests, that are untouched by humans.

Index

FEB - - 2010